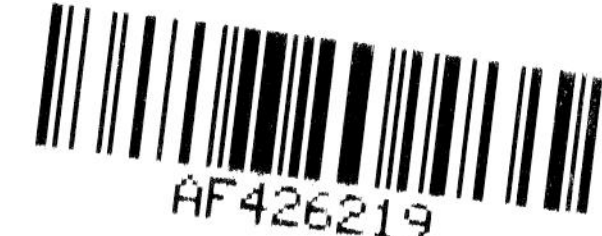

The Little Boy Who Thought

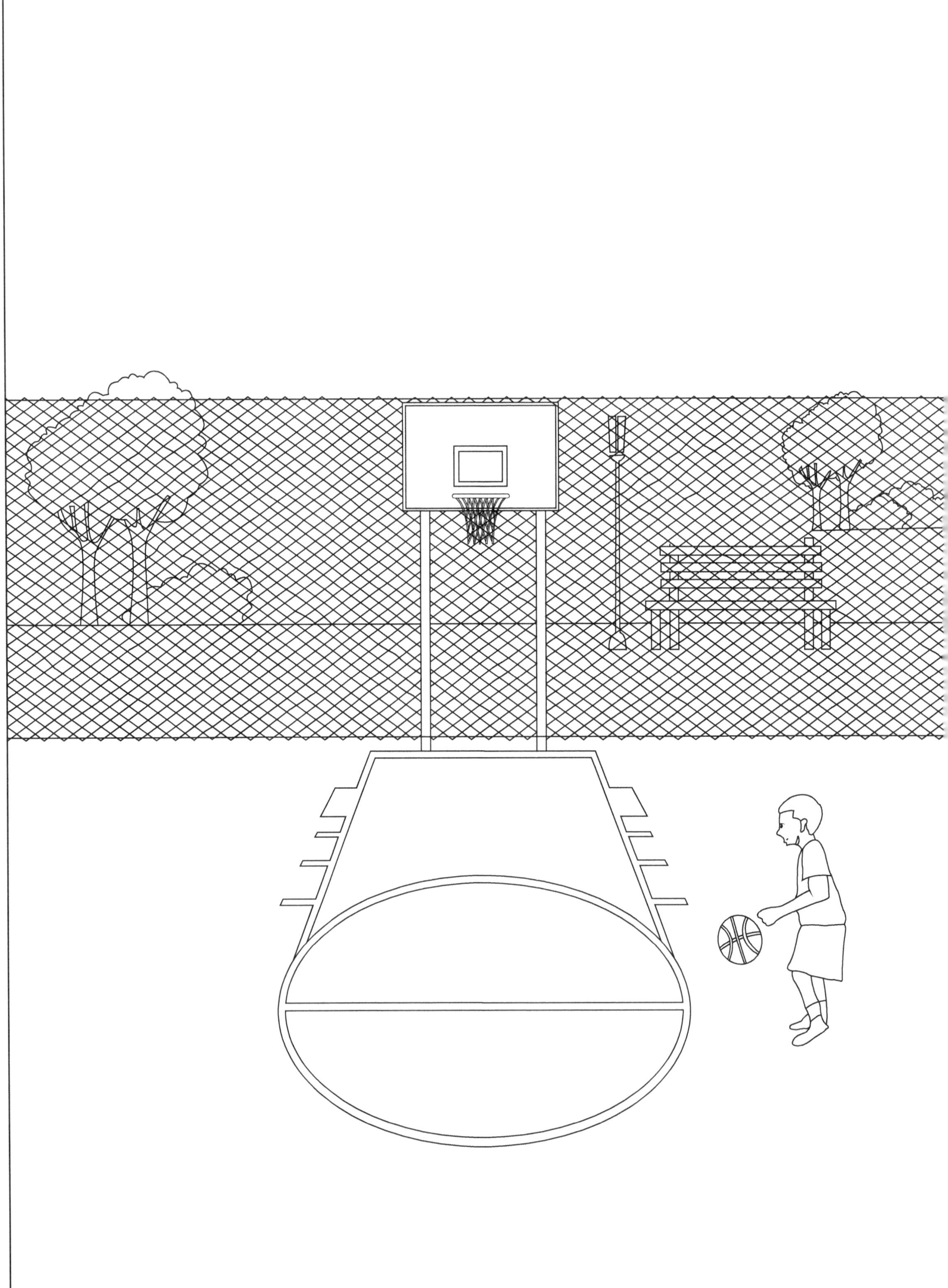

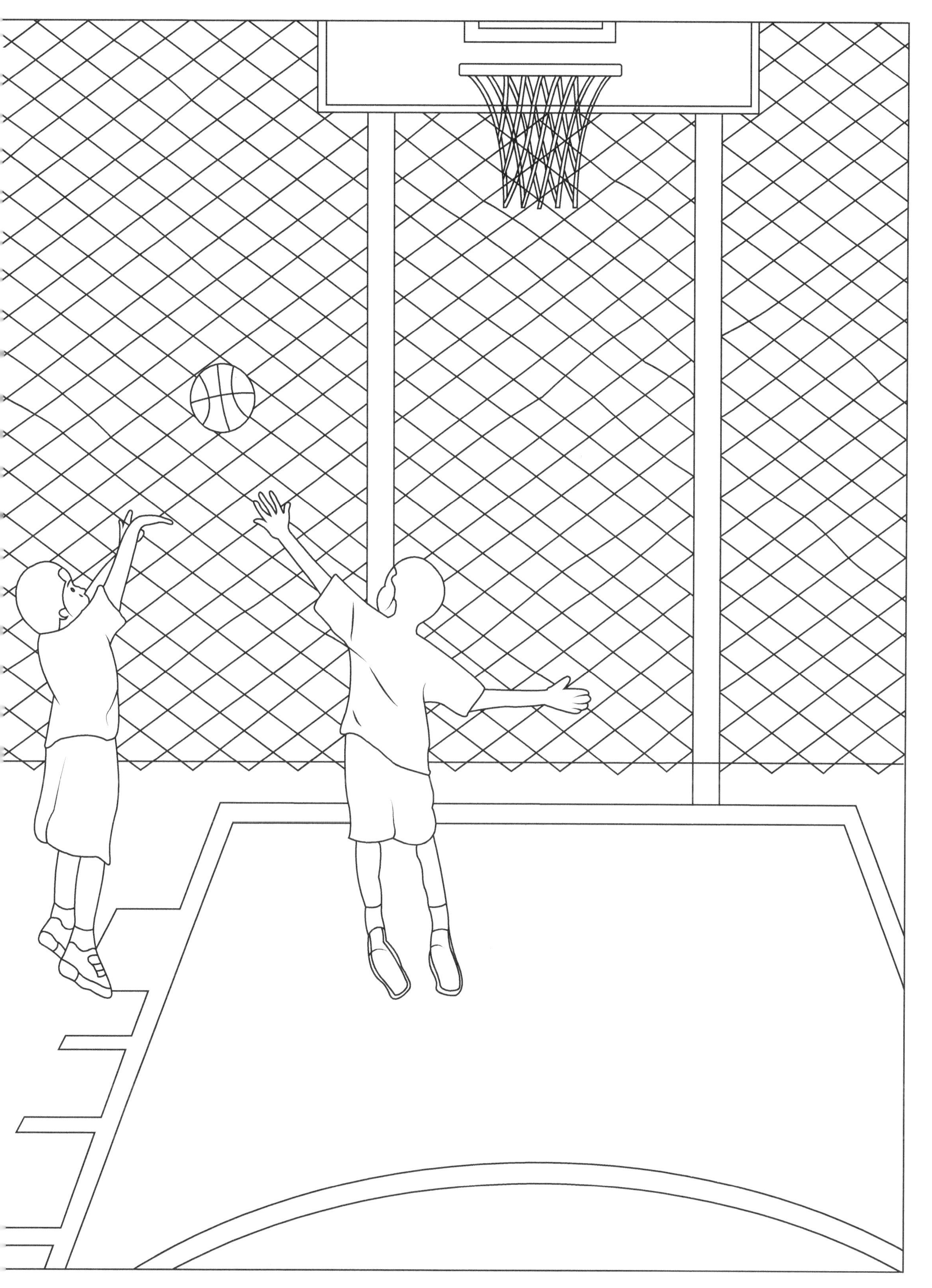

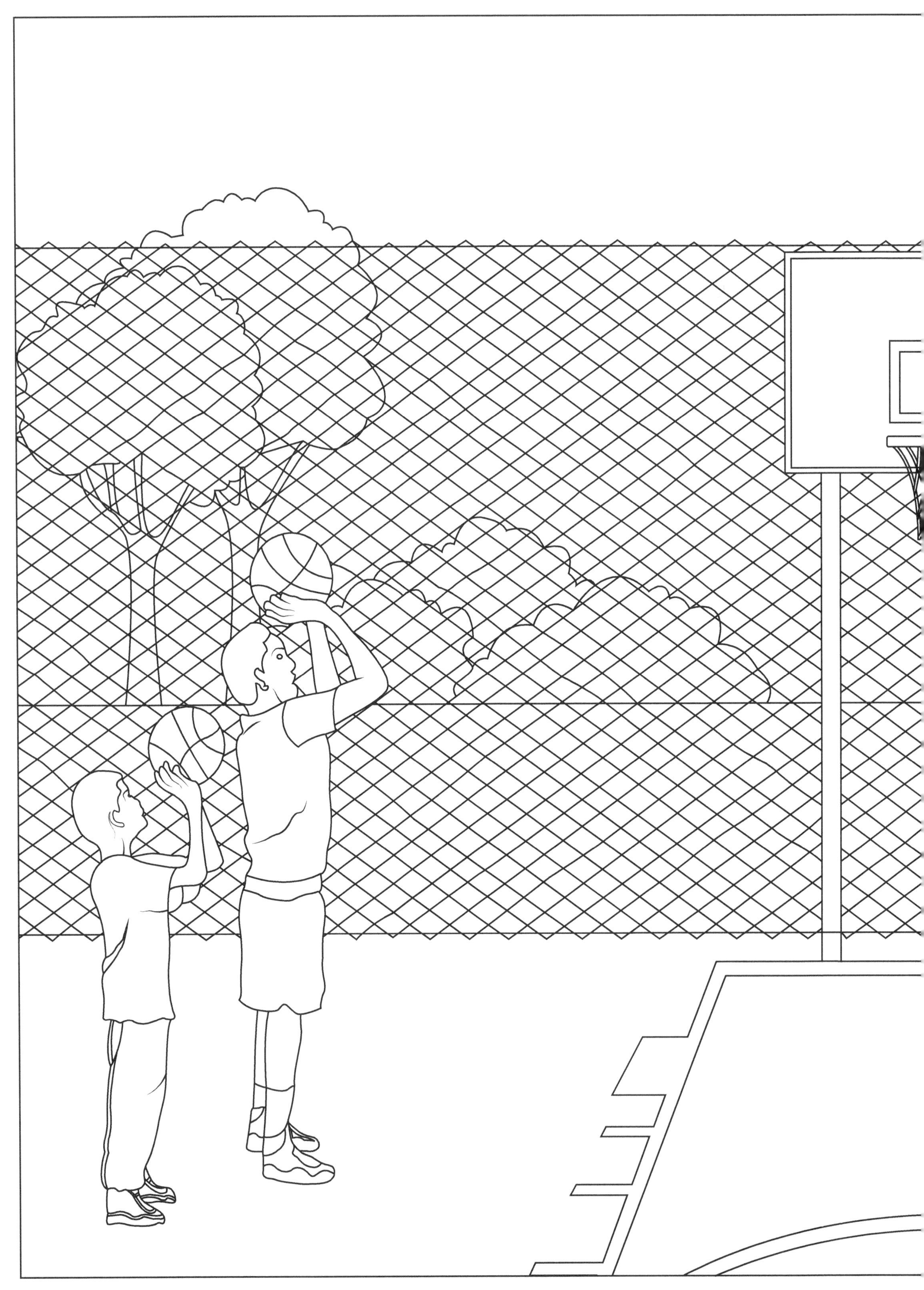

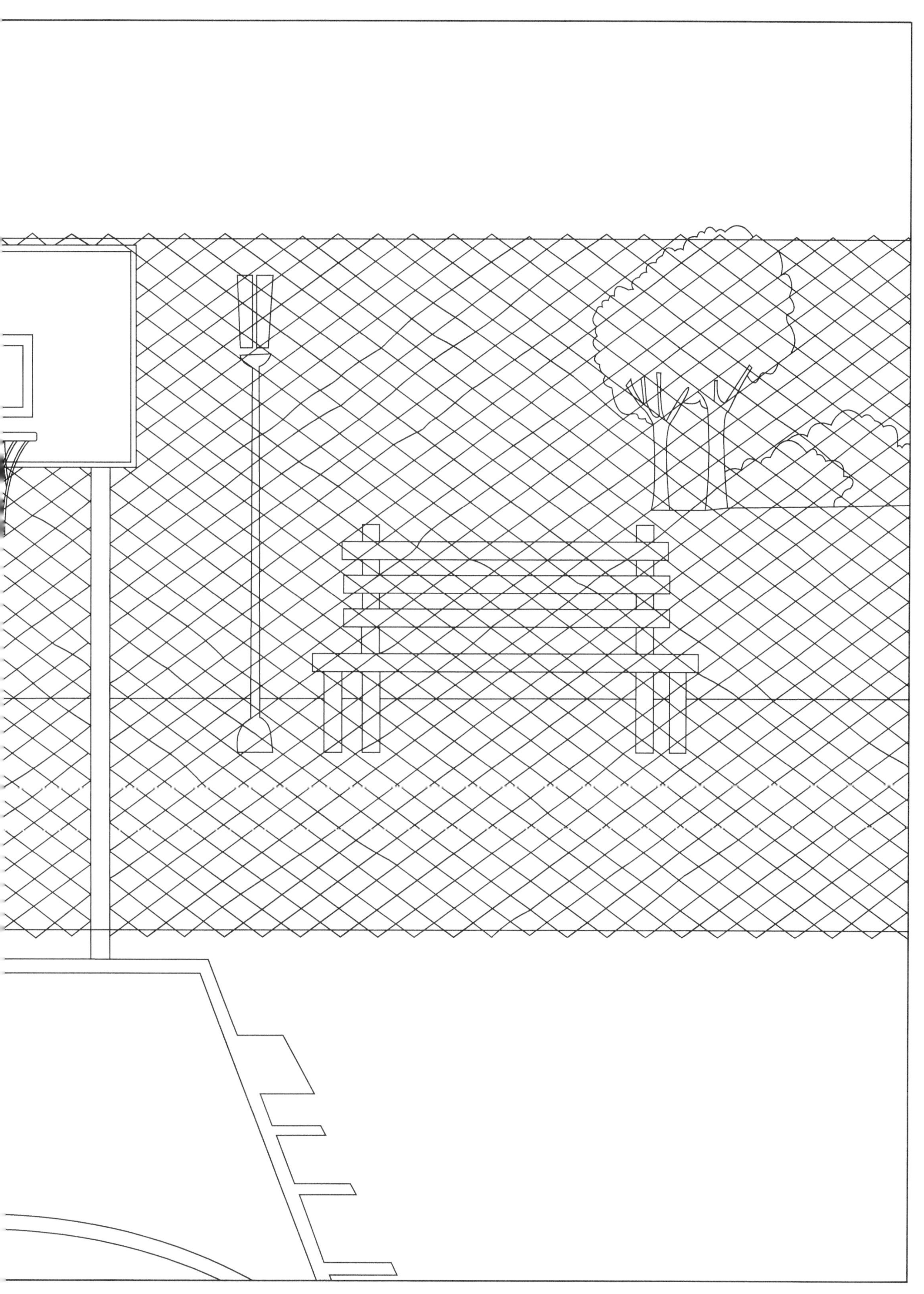

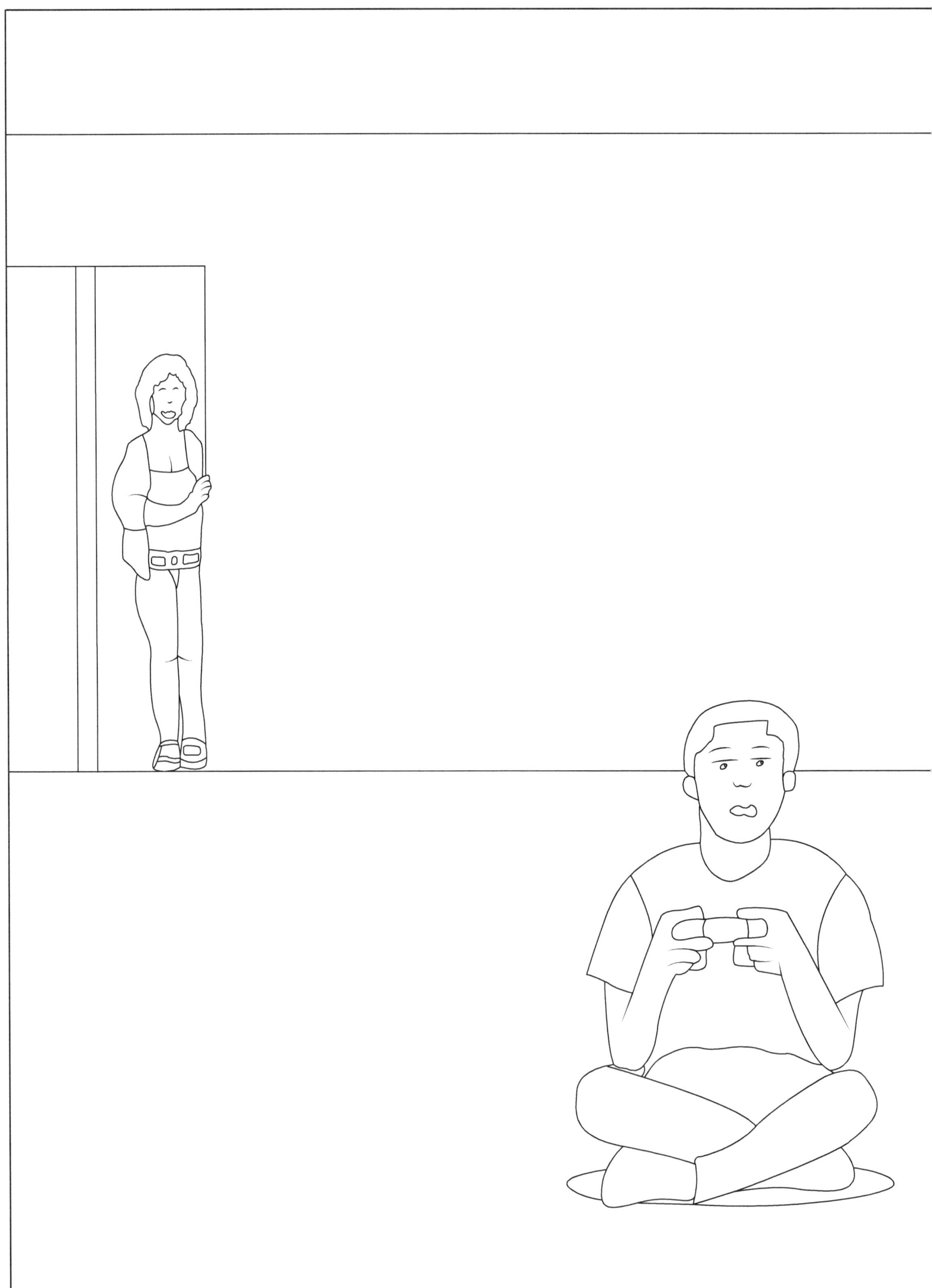

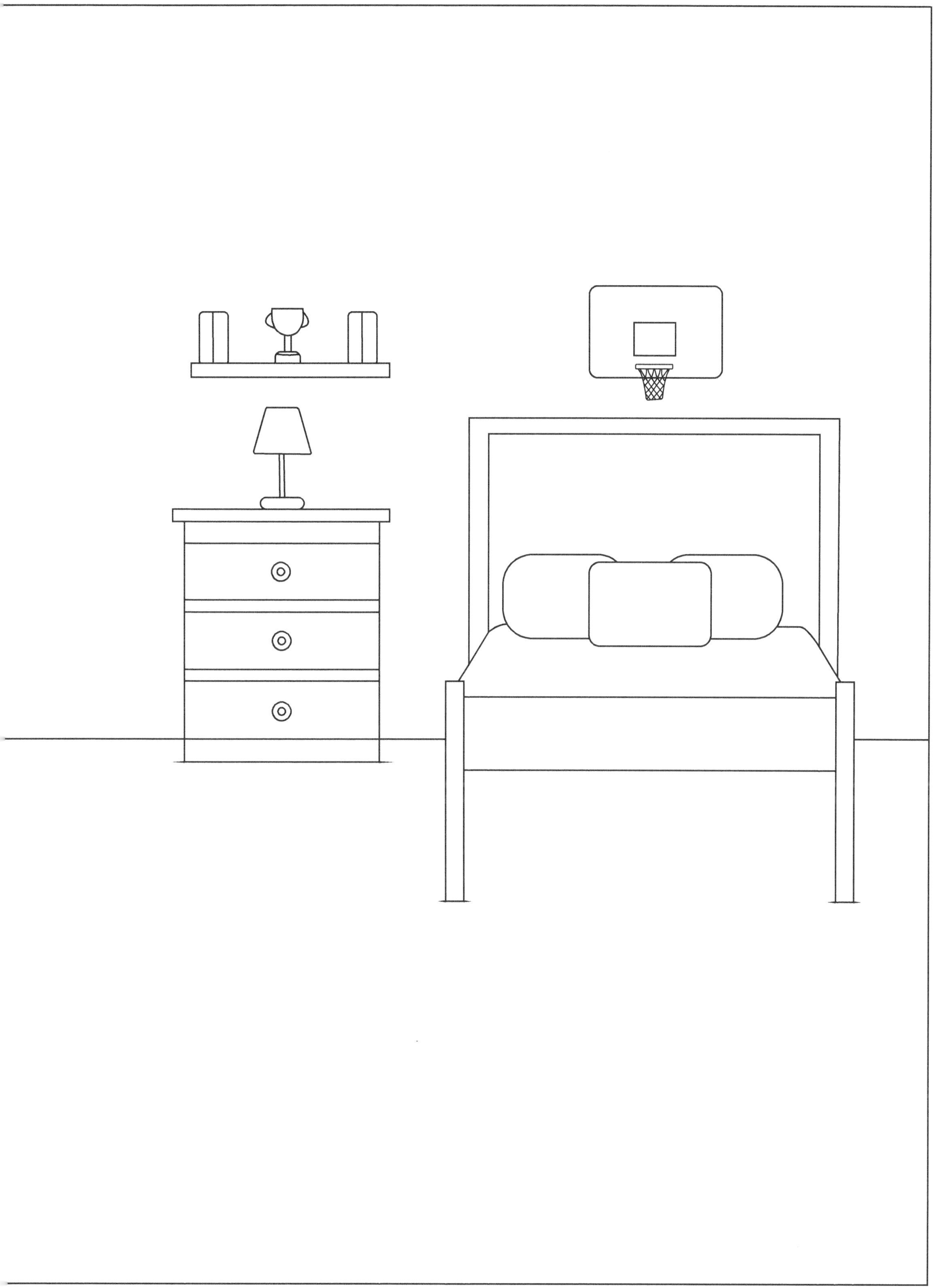

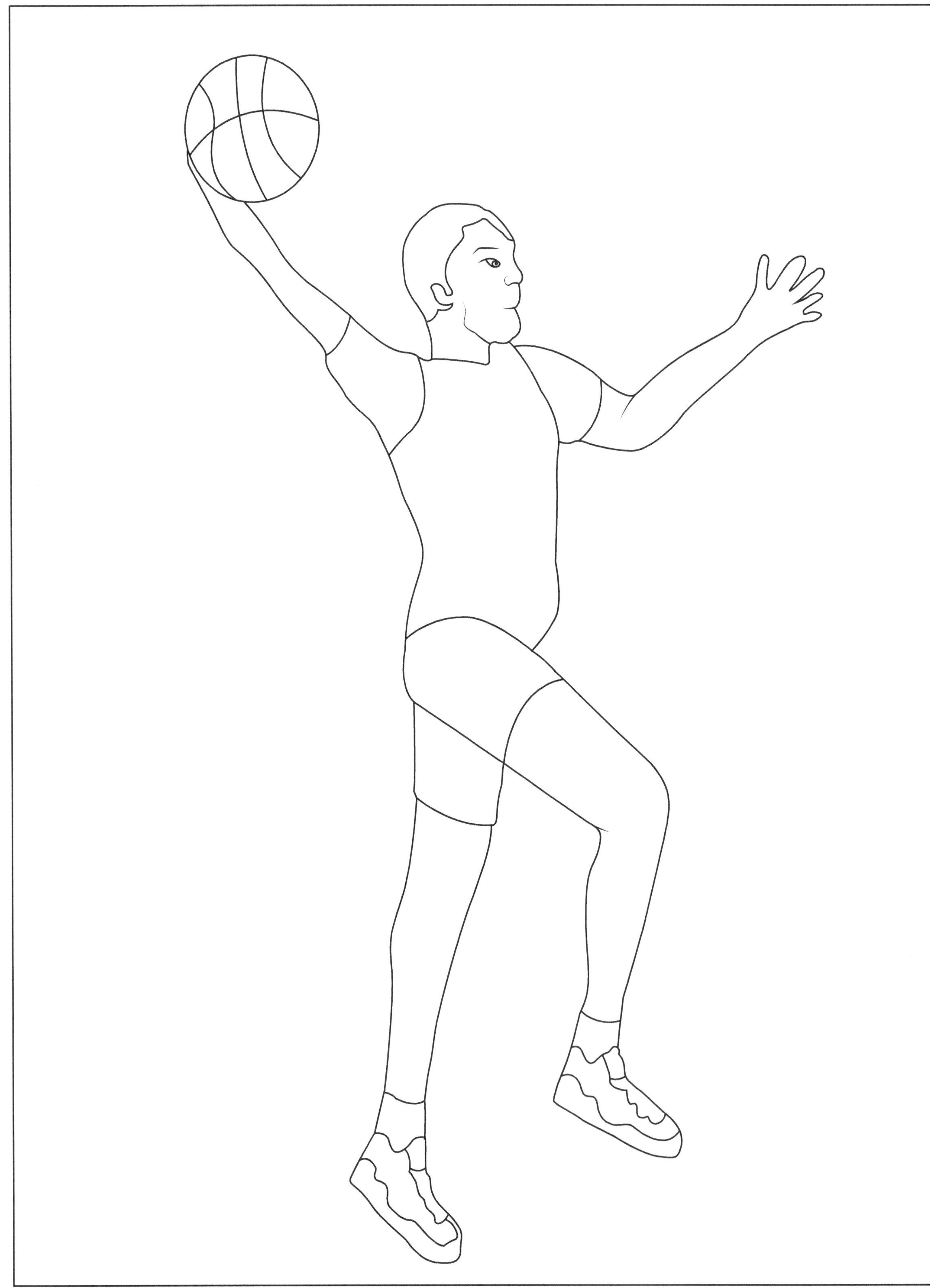

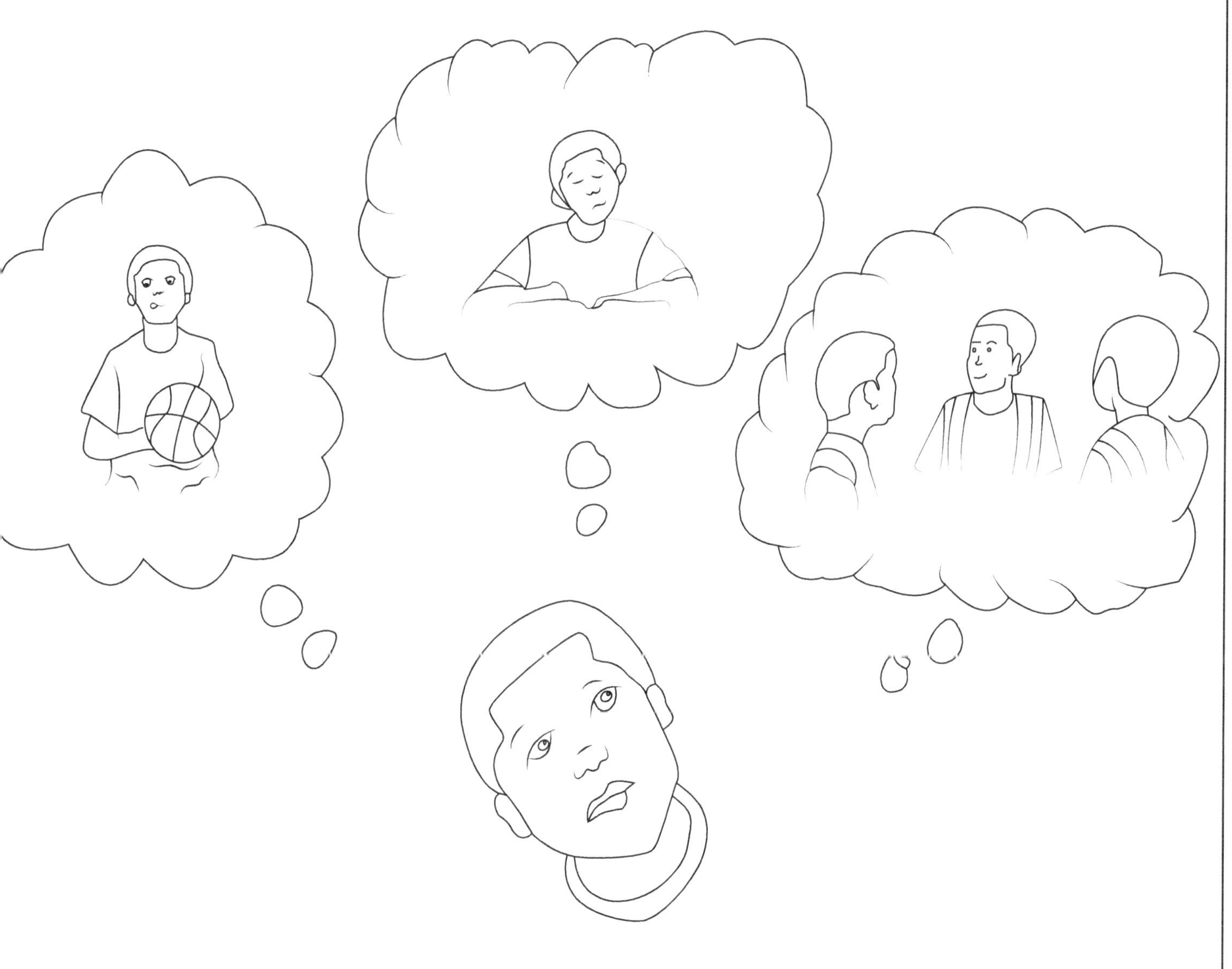

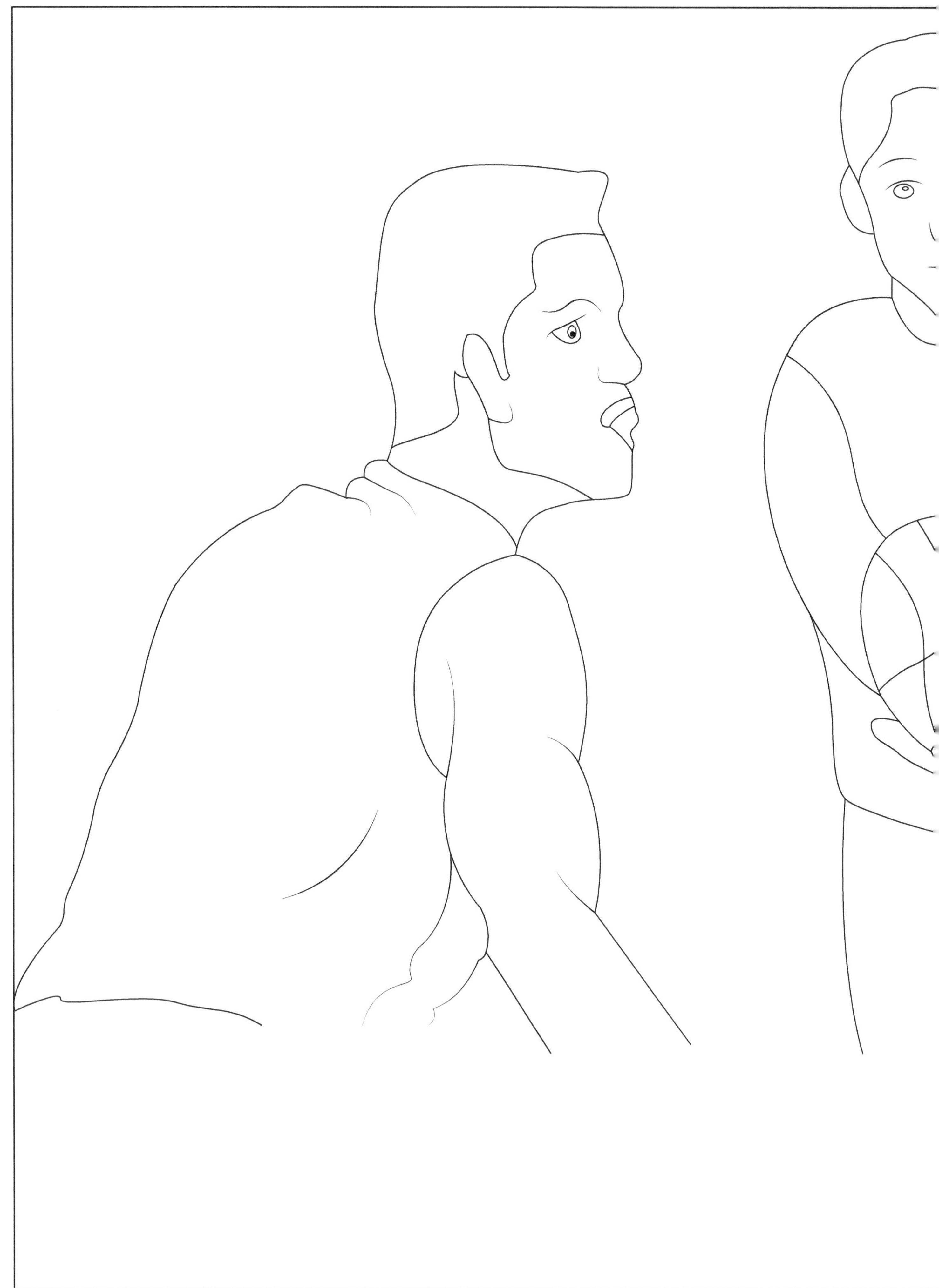

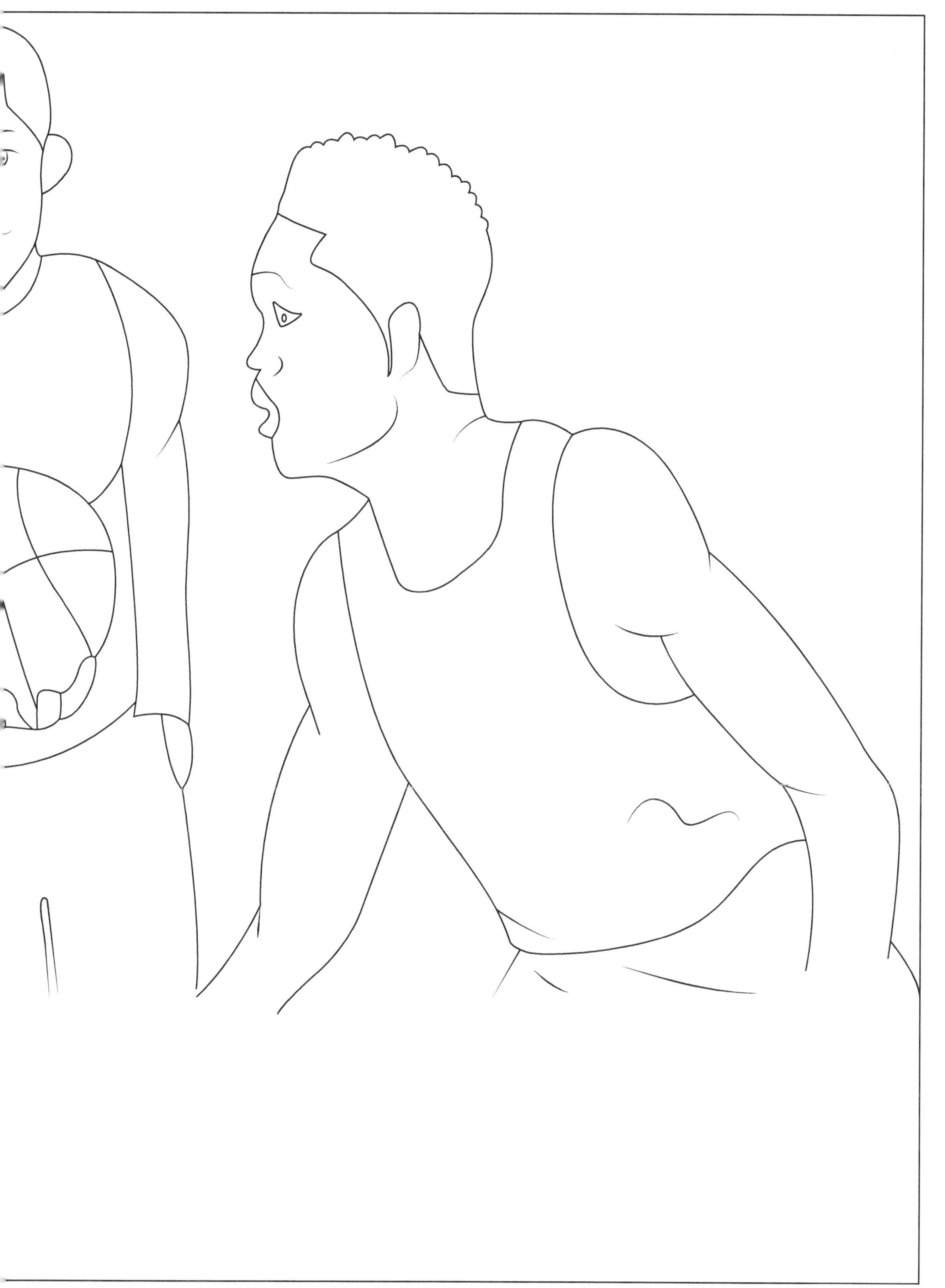

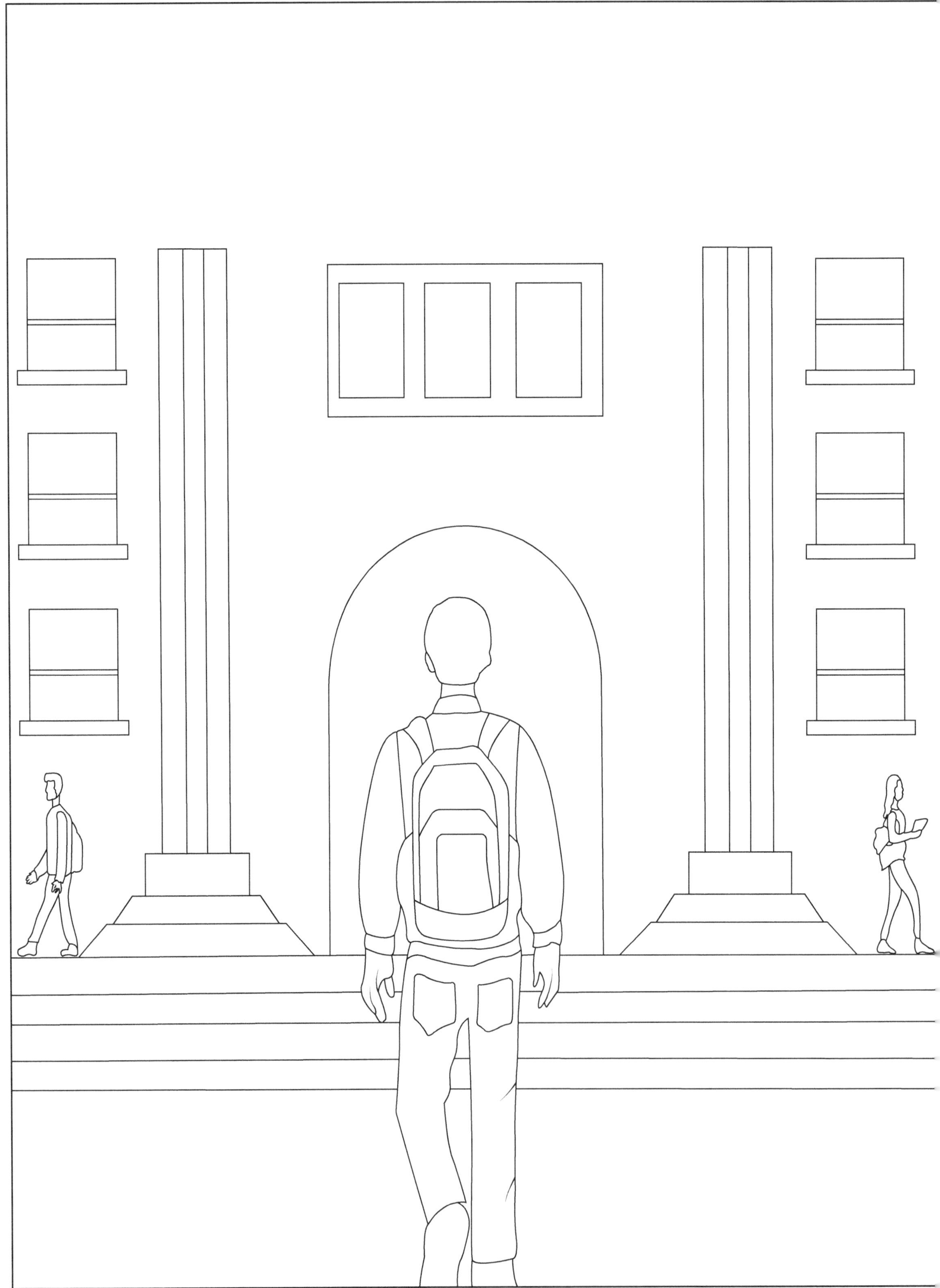

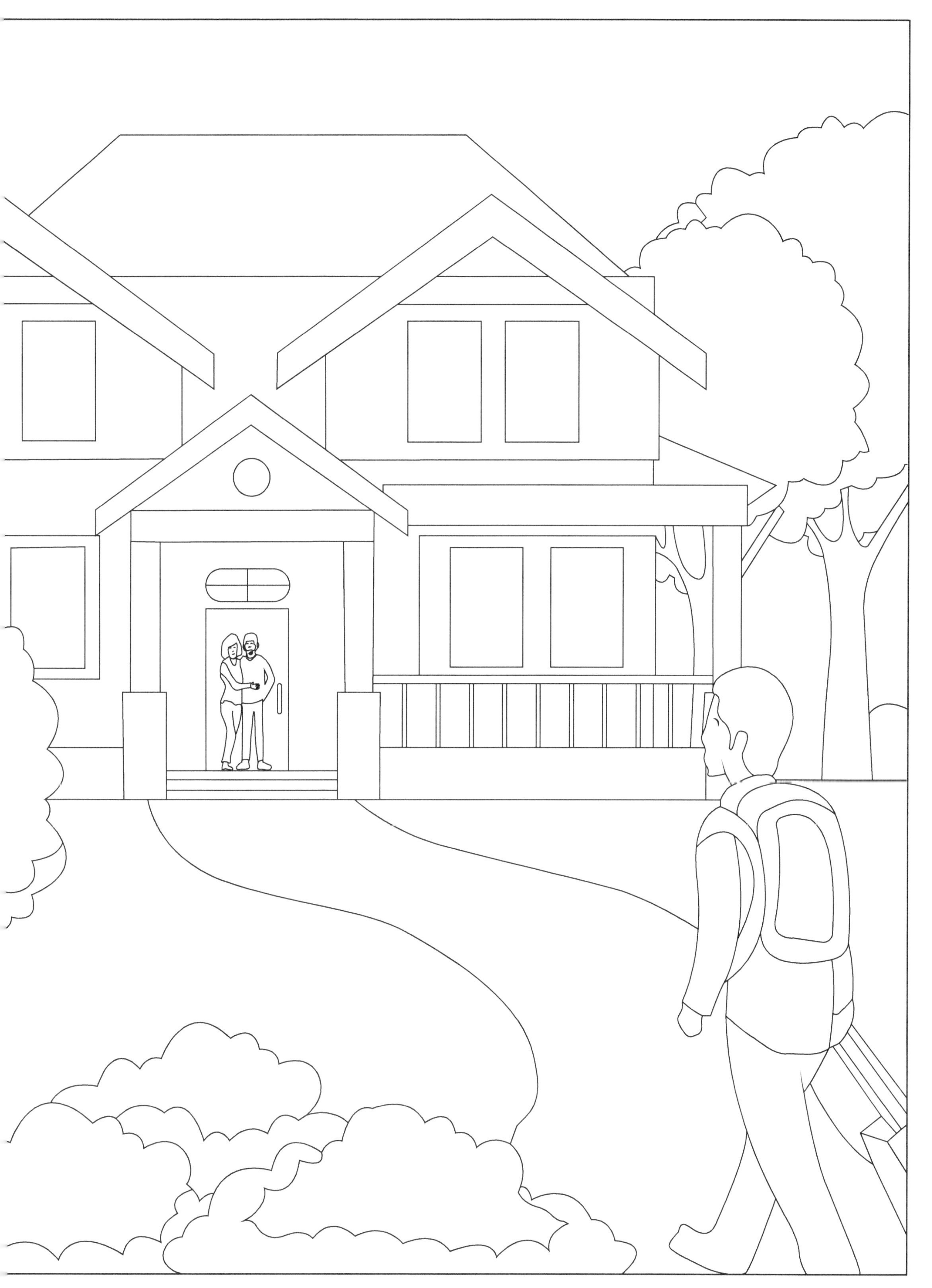

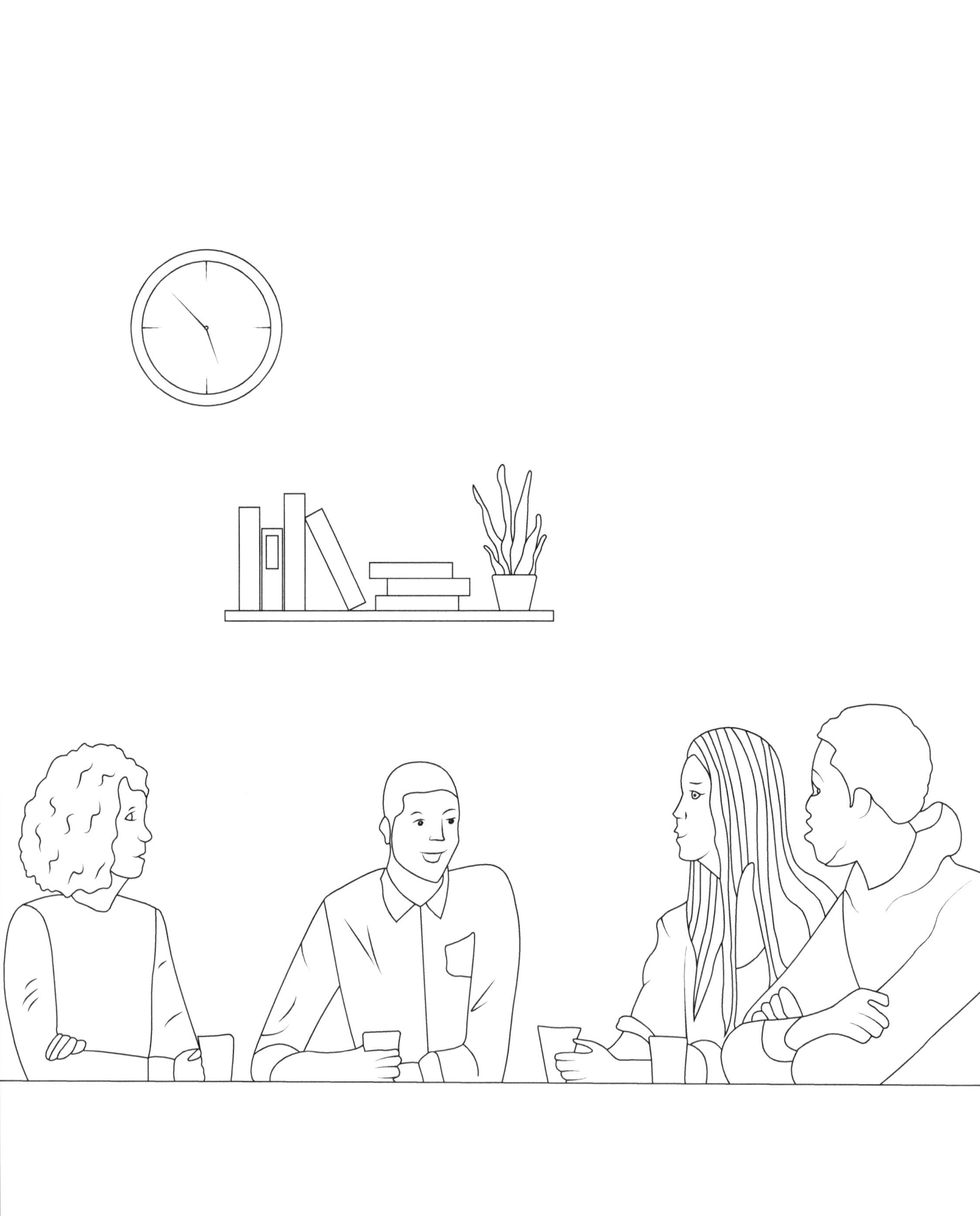

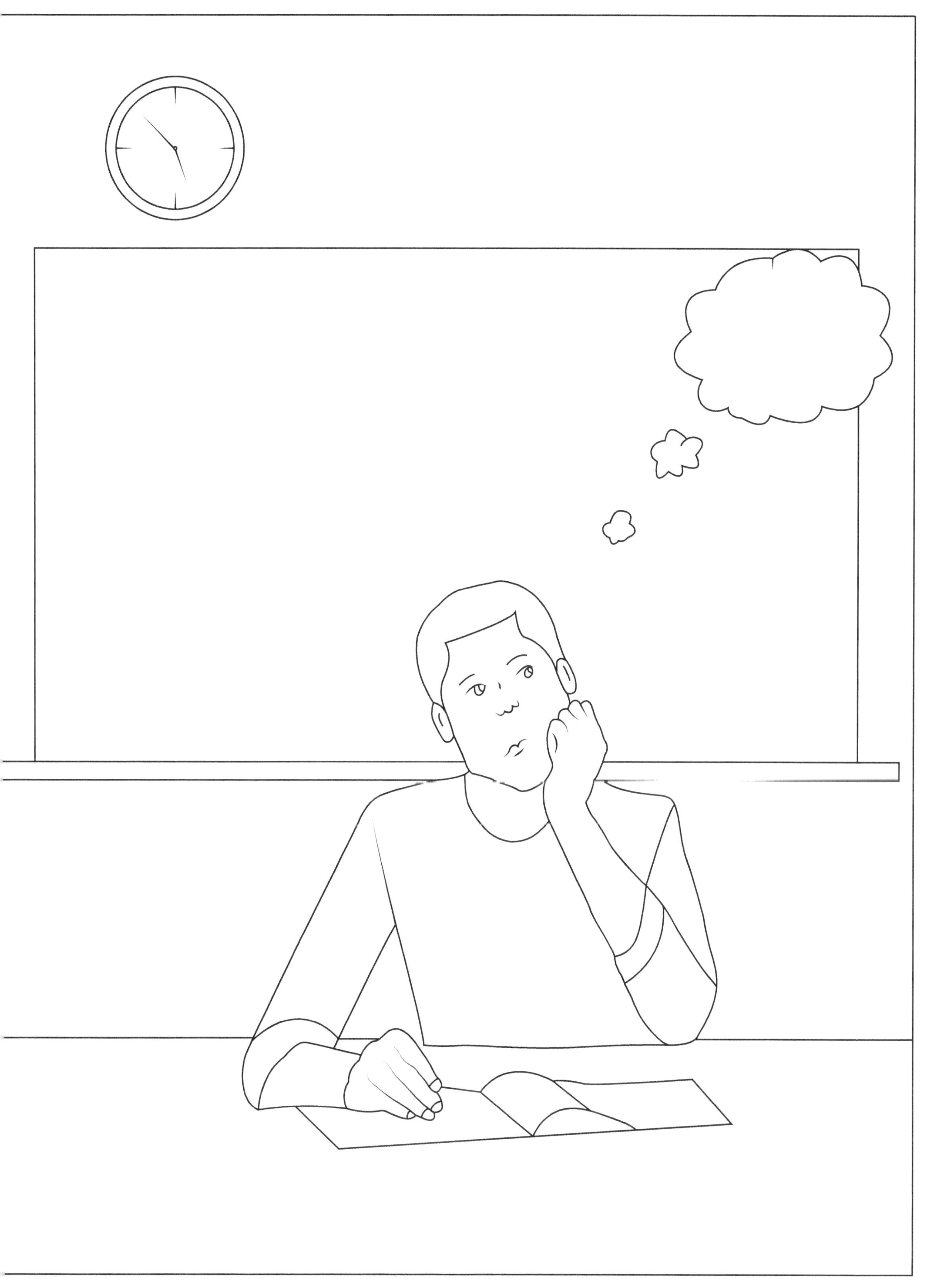

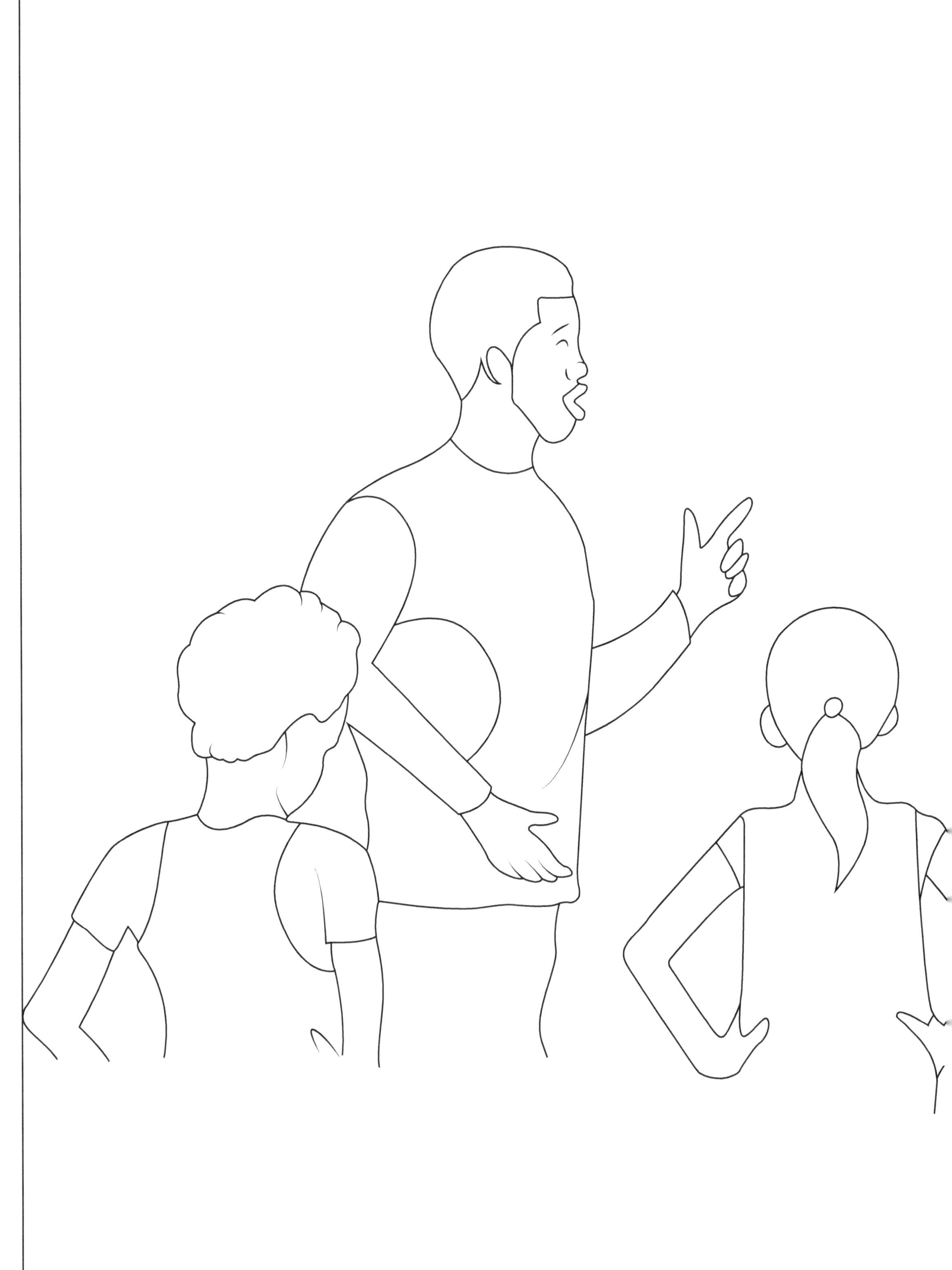

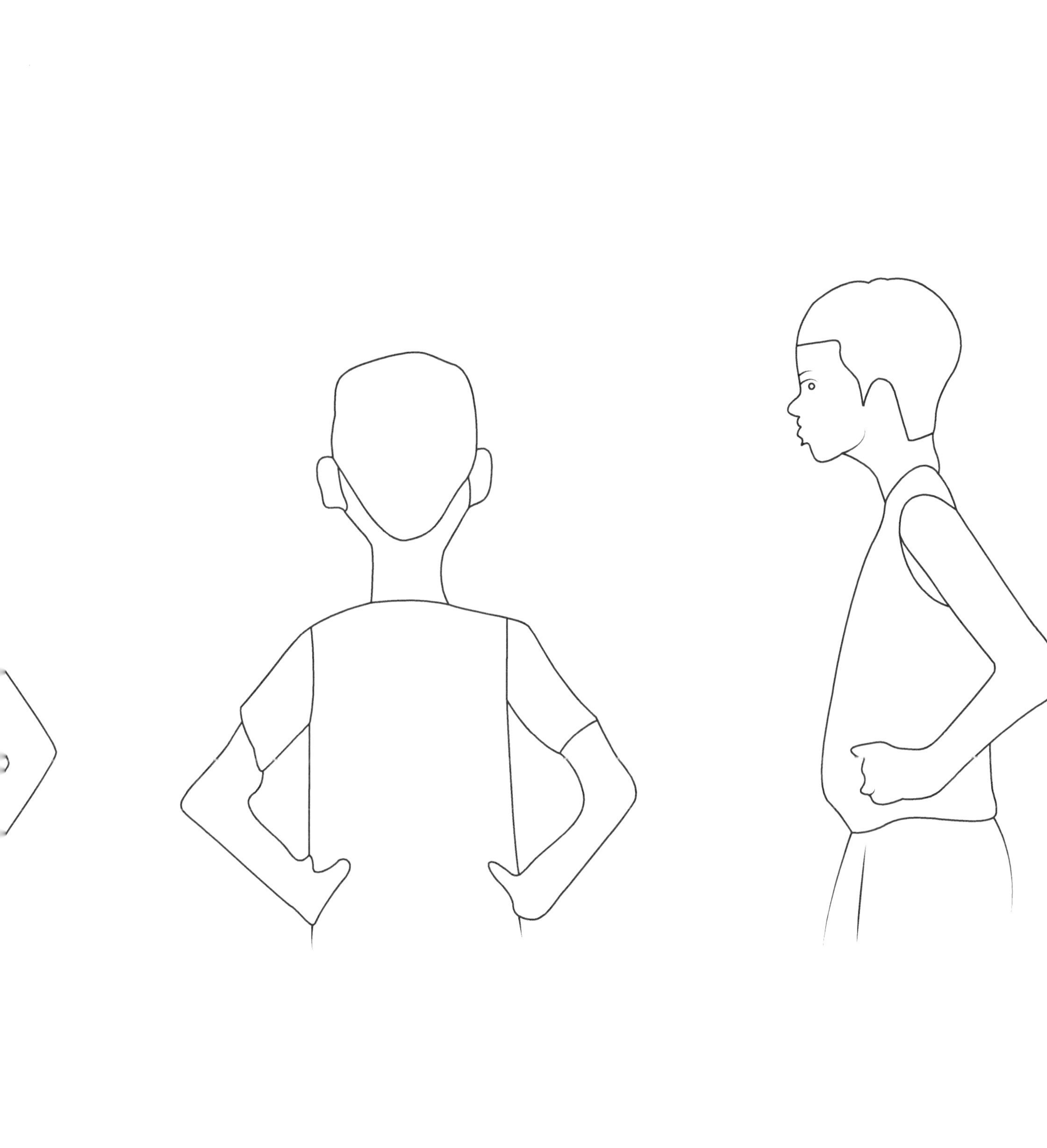

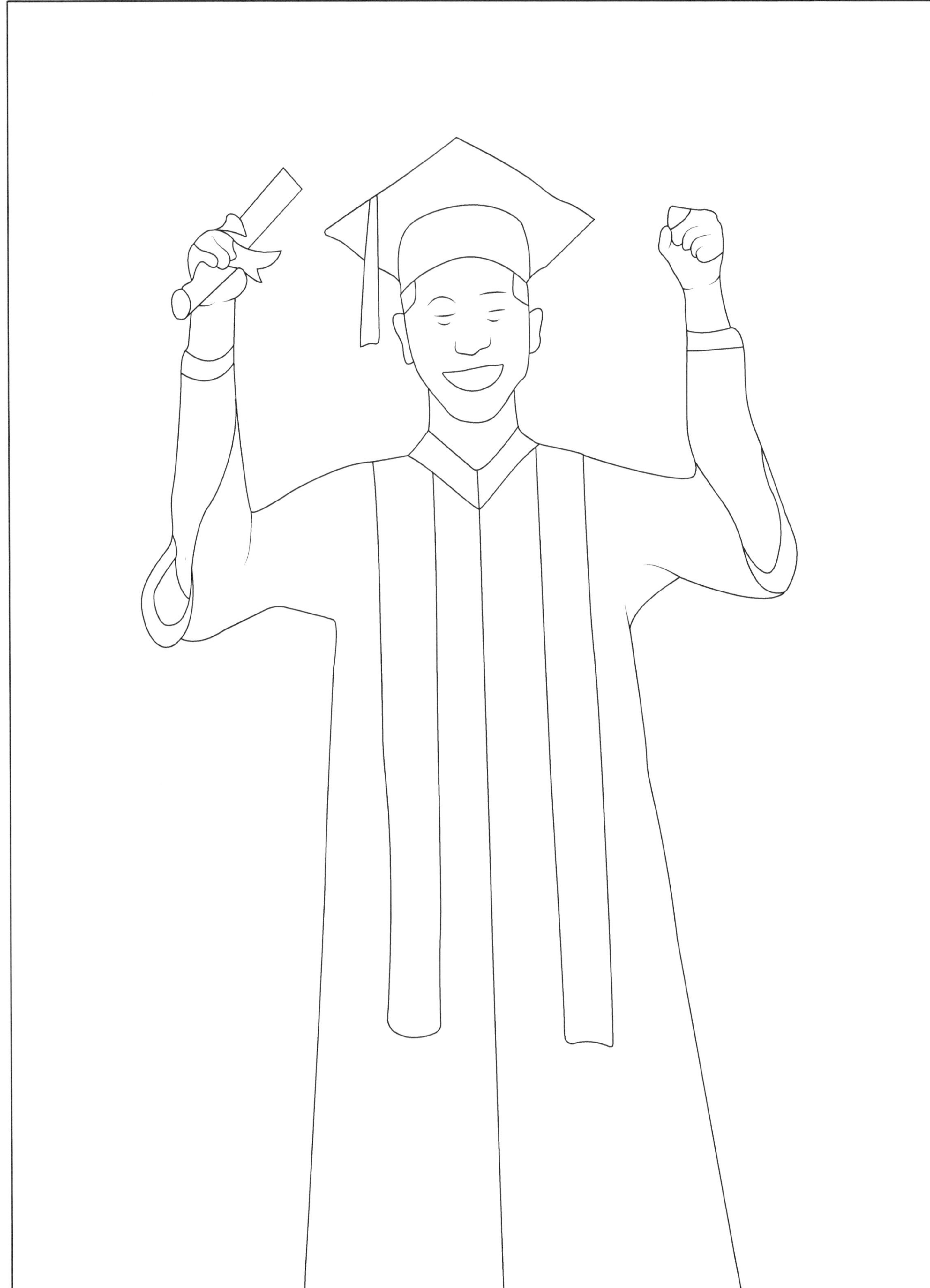

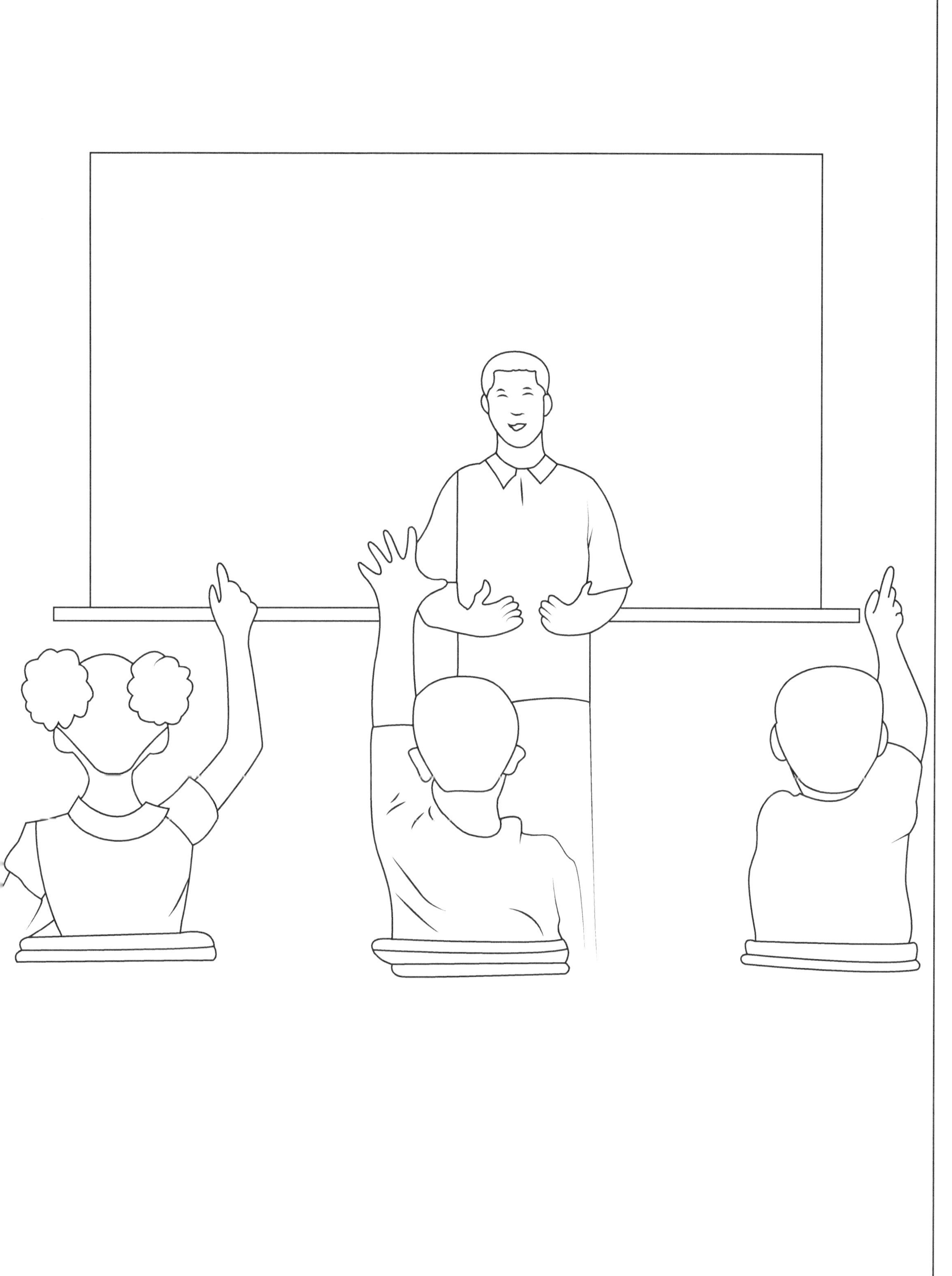

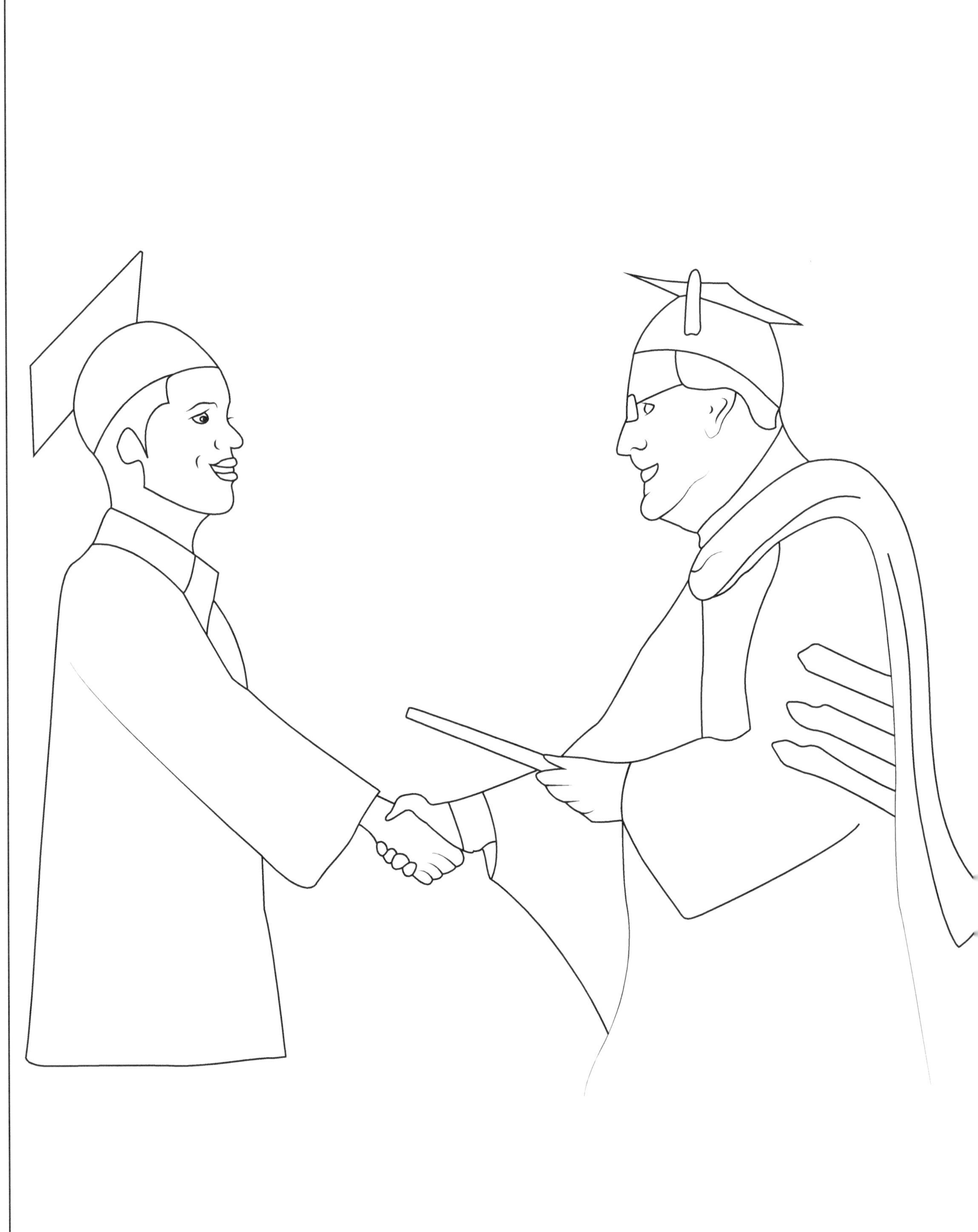

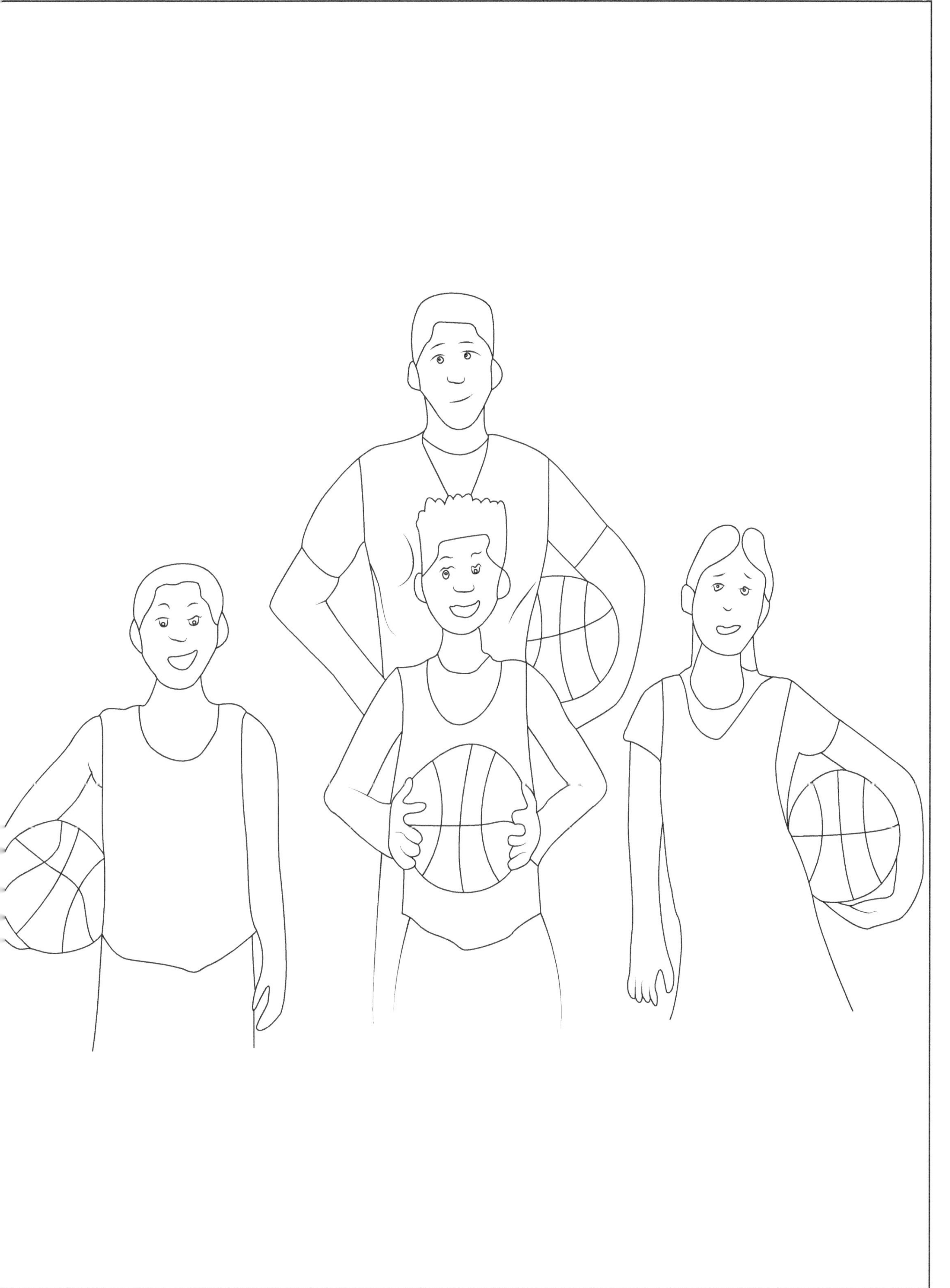

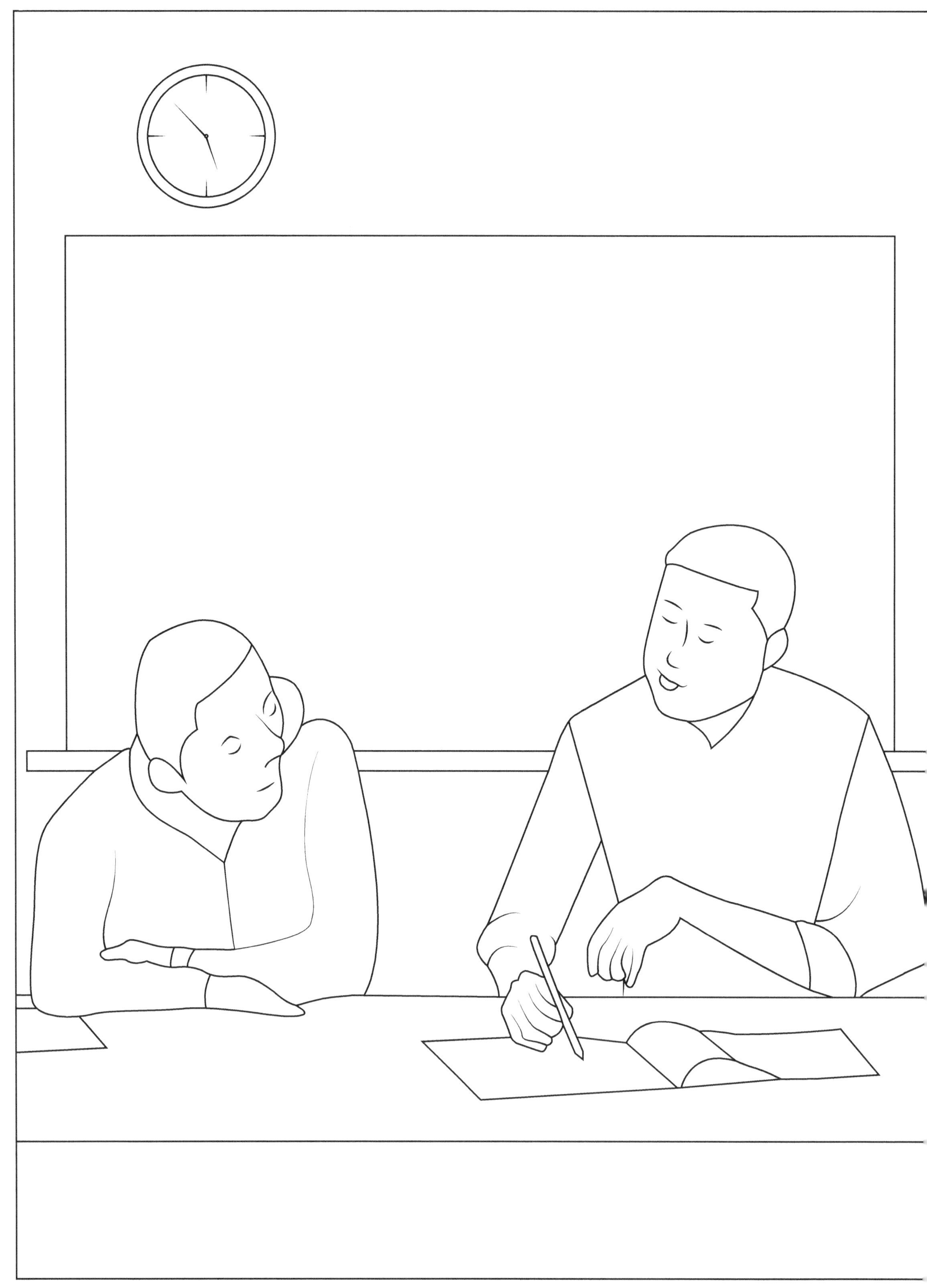

Share your thoughts